(previous page 1)
Bluejoint reedgrass

(Cover and previous pages 2-3)

Late evening came on this September day with a warmth which brushed across the Lamar Valley in the light of the autumn sun. The days were now shorter than the nights, but the heat from the long summer days was still present on the land. The broad welcoming expanse of the valley is embraced by Specimen Ridge to the right and the high snowy peaks of Saddle and Little Saddle Mountains in the distance to the left. The thick stands of grass and aspen, cottonwood, and evergreen trees had completed a vigorous healthy growing season and were now standing in the fullness of the year.

(opposite)

Just a few minutes after sunrise, while the light was warm, this cow moose was browsing near Floating Island Lake.

For no apparent reason, she put her ears back and ran down the slope into the rising sunlight. She ran fast for about 200 yards as if she were late for something, then stopped abruptly and went back to browsing in a boggy place containing her favorite leaves. She didn't look back as if something had been chasing her or had startled her. She didn't have to race me to get to her food, so I don't know why she thought the sudden short run was necessary.

THE COMFORT *of* AUTUMN

THE SEASONS OF YELLOWSTONE

by Tom Murphy

Crystal Creek Press

THE SEASONS OF YELLOWSTONE

The Comfort of Autumn is the second of a four-volume set by Tom Murphy called *The Seasons of Yellowstone.* The turning of a full year in Yellowstone Park gives us four distinct seasons. Each one overlaps and flows into the next one but has its own unique character.

Spring's uniqueness comes from the powerful pulse of light warming the land. It starts and maintains the growth of vegetation and supports the birth of a myriad of creatures.

Summer is defined by the growth of the wildlife and the luxuriant leaves, flowers, grasses, and forbs. The long warm days and cool nights make it the most pleasant and easy season.

Autumn brings maturation and independence for the young animals, the rut and mating season for many large mammals, and the drive to put on fat for the coming winter. It is the time for the seeding of plants and starting the process of dormancy for trees, bushes, grasses, and forbs.

In winter the struggle to endure and survive the harshest weather of the year is evident in every part of Yellowstone. It is the season of simple, quiet, clean beauty. Snow sweeps over the landscape reforming the land into smoother and softer shapes while the cold, at the same time, is brittle and sharp.

Please send us your name and address if you would like to be notified when future volumes are released.

All photographs in this book are available as archival giclée prints.

Crystal Creek Press, 402 South 5th Street, Livingston MT 59047 406 222 2302

Published in 2005 by Crystal Creek Press
Livingston, Montana

Book design by Adrienne Pollard
Printed and bound in China by C & C Offset Printing Co., Ltd.

ISBN 0-9668619-3-0 (clothbound)

Autumn is a
second spring
when every leaf
is a flower.

—ALBERT CAMUS
writer and philosopher
(1913-1960)

Autumn is the season of completion. It brings the end of the annual growth of many plants and the fruition and death of many more. It signals the transition to the dormancy of winter and surrounds all the animals in a comforting time of warmth and wild abundance. Beautiful forms have the same life in every season so the deaths are not tragic if they contribute to the next generation's vitality.

Annual plants should have grown and produced a surplus of seeds by autumn to have fulfilled their place in the community of life. Perennials should have at least survived with enough strength left to carry them through the coming winter. Ideally they should have produced seeds and strengthened their root systems, stems and branches.

The vibrant and varied colors of vegetation unique to autumn appear only after the overpowering green chlorophyll evaporates. In the furious push to grow, replicate and reproduce, the engines of life in green plants are driven by the surge of chlorophyll. Underneath this green all along is the color of the basic structure of the plants. Only after the completion of this growth and the abandonment of the mask of chlorophyll are their true colors revealed.

Most insects have laid eggs or entered into a larval stage in autumn to carry their species through the winter. The uncounted multitudes from summer, left after the reproductive cycle is completed, will mostly die.

There are many ways for animals to succeed. They may prepare for hibernation, and accumulate fat reserves, they may store food in secure places for future winter consumption, or they may migrate away from their summer range. This migration may be only a few miles to higher or lower elevations or it may be thousands of miles, even to Central or South America.

Hibernation is primarily an autumn activity because all the vital preparation must be done then. Bears hibernate and take their young cubs with them. Marmots, chipmunks and others hibernate, but the young are not snuggled and helped the next spring.

(Above) Spreading dogbane

Den location and preparation must be accomplished well before winter sets in. The lush vegetation that grew all spring, summer, and autumn is available at the peak of biomass in autumn. The winter sleep of hibernation is anticlimactic. I suspect the winter dreams during hibernation are those of plenty in the perfect days of autumn.

Most birds and mammals eat extra food, as much food as they can, in a survival response called hyperphasia. This accumulation of fat hopefully gives them the reserve energy to migrate, hibernate or endure. Some store food in caches to be assured of adequate nutrition over the winter. Beaver cache branches under water, Clark's nutcrackers hide pine nuts in the ground, pika build haystacks in talus slopes, and squirrels store a variety of food items from mushrooms to seeds in trees and underground.

Young animals achieve a new independence in autumn. Juvenile elk, coyote, and otter are a few of the creatures that are weaned from their mother's milk and have to acquire their own food, but they stay with either their mother or with other adults to learn how to survive winter. The autumn transition of total dependence to total independence or group interdependence is a critical learning stage in these animals' success.

The beginnings of independence are most evident in birds and predators. Some birds are entirely on their own a few weeks after they leave the nest. Their mortality rates are high because they are naive about the many risks of life. The bright and the lucky will live. Some birds stay near the adults and learn to migrate or learn how to hunt in the forgiving lushness of autumn.

It is fun to watch these juveniles learning the possibilities of our big, complex world. I have watched a young coyote puzzling over how to dig out a ground squirrel. I have seen wolf pups chase four bull elk and then realize an elk can be dangerous when the bulls spin around and with eight multi-pointed antlers start to chase them back.

For predators there are many awkward and potentially injurious misses while pursuing food. If an individual doesn't learn quickly enough to be a successful hunter, autumn will be its last season. The highest mortality rates of animals come in the first days or months after they separate from their mothers and many separate in autumn.

For most adults it is the end of their responsibilities as parents and a time of freedom to rest, recuperate, and to put on weight and regain their strength for winter. It is a time of relaxation. This is when most animals achieve their maximum health and strength, so they look their best. They are fat, strong, fast and sleek.

There is a delicate lightness in each individual life in relationship to the whole universe, yet each unique life contributes something important to the unified force of all existence. Autumn is the season when life can be at rest in comfortable peace in life's constantly spinning push to appear and grow. It is a time when the earth can take a deep breath and show off its colors, when the bison cow can play as she did when she was a calf.

The elk mating season or rut occurs in September. Their high-pitched whistle or "bugle" is a surprising sound coming from such a large animal. The bugling is a challenging or defiant call to other bulls, telling them—"I am here, I am strong, I am in charge." Bugling actually includes a variety of calls: grunts, popping sounds, whistling, and deep moans. Male elk urinate on the ground, roll in the dirt and mud, rake their antlers across the ground and through grass and small trees, using up much of their energy for more than a month. Thus the most aggressive bulls lose a lot of sleep and weight. If there is an early, hard winter, these bulls will be some of the first to winter kill. It seems counterproductive for them to be among those most likely to die; but, these strong bulls should have many of their genes successfully living on in the upcoming spring crop of calves.

Foraging along the banks
of the Yellowstone
River, this black bear
scrambled up and over
and around these huge
granite boulders eating
rose hips and leafy
plants which seemed
to be the primary
reward for his work.

The route he took in the maze of rock
and brush seemed to be completely
random except that he slowly wandered
down the valley.

There are relatively few
brightly colored trees in
Yellowstone in the autumn.

The primary fall color is yellow, and it
usually comes from trees of the genus
Populus, which includes cottonwoods
and the smaller aspen or quaking aspen.
The scattered stands of aspen are mostly
around the northern range. *Populus
tremuloides,* the Latin name for aspen,
comes from the easy fluttering of the
leaves on their slender stems even on
apparently still days.

Juniper wood is resistant to
decay and in the dry, cold
semi-arid environment of the
Lamar Valley even small twigs
will survive for many years.

A juniper branch had grown out across
this lichen and moss covered rock and
while it was alive had created a shaded
micro environment for the colonies of
lichen. After the juniper branch died,
the splayed fingers of the durable twigs
lay across the miniature landscape of the
rock, a dendritic shape mimicking a
stream channel.

Northern black currant is
a common shrub in the
Yellowstone ecosystem
that exhibits bright red
leaves in autumn.

Preferring moist mountain slopes
along streams and in timber, it
is not particularly noticeable in
other seasons.

Antlers exist only
on a small group
of ruminants
which are all in
the deer family.

This family called Cervidae, includes deer,
elk, caribou, and moose. The antlers are
grown and shed annually and are made of
a bone like material. During the growth
phase, from early spring to late summer, the
antlers contain a complex of blood vessels
and are covered with a short dense hair
called velvet. When the antlers are completely grown, the blood vessels die back.
The bony material hardens and dries, and
the velvet splits and is rubbed off. The
palmated antlers of this bull moose still have
some residual red stains from the old blood
vessels and a few remnants of the velvet on
the right tips. Soon he will have rubbed all
the velvet off and covered the antlers with
pitch and dirt so they will be brown, yet
the tips will be polished clean and white.

Fall weather in Yellowstone will often include snow showers.

The air temperature can be above freezing, though wet snowflakes cascade down to the still unfrozen ground, melting quickly. These two small lines of aspen trees were about three hundred yards away. A 500 mm lens compressed the foreground sage, the middle ground of the lines of aspens, and the background of conifers. The falling snow softened the colors and textures of the elements of this image and at the same time created a pattern of short diagonal lines.

The cottontail rabbit gets its common name from the small, white fuzzy tail that looks like a cotton ball.

There is speculation that this white, fuzzy object bobs along erratically when the rabbit runs, making it more difficult for a predator to catch it. Rabbits, hares and pika are the three members of the lagomorph order. Rabbits' young are born helpless, naked, and with their eyes stuck shut for several days like kittens or puppies. This cottontail rabbit was resting in a small hollowed out spot under some grass, which provided visual cover from predators, both in the air and on the ground.

A thick stand of goldenrod
was growing in the damp
ground beneath the aspens
along Crystal Creek.

Goldenrod's genus name, *Solidago,*
means to make whole, referring to the
healing properties of the plant. Different
species across the country have been used
as medicines for "strengthening the brain,"
and as an antidote for rattlesnake bite, a
treatment for sores and cuts and for
headaches. Thomas Edison spent time
researching a couple of species to determine
if they might be a commercial source for
rubber. The late evening sun backlit the
pale yellow flowers while I was walking
back from a day on Specimen Ridge
through the large stand of mature aspen.

While lying on my
back in the shade
of this grove I realized
I was working after
all because I noticed
this new perspective
of the yellow branches
scattered up the
white trunks.

The aspens appeared to be leaning

down from the sky towards me.

Trees, along with all other plants, prefer specific soil conditions, seasonal moisture levels, temperature variations and cycles, direct or indirect sunlight, and a vast array of other requirements.

Sometimes they need other plants to shelter their seedlings. Sometimes they need insects or mammals to disperse their seeds. We only partly understand this community of life. The more we learn, it seems, the more connected, dynamic, and complex we find that it all is, and the more we realize how little we know. Aspen, Douglas fir, lodge-pole pine and Engleman spruce usually grow in distinct areas, but here on Crystal Bench in the Lamar Valley they are mixed more than usual. One thing we can say for sure is that they make a beautiful mixture of color and texture.

Folds in the northern grassy slopes of Specimen Ridge create micro climates where trees and brush are able to thrive.

The small draws catch and hold the snow and provide a sheltered cool place for the vegetation to grow. The exposed drier slopes are left to the grass communities. Amethyst Creek flows north through the deepest fold here in the center of this image

A small herd of bison cows and calves walked up the slope from Crystal Bench to the old Bannock Trail along the northern base of Specimen Ridge.

We have named this travel corridor after some relatively recent human use, when in reality the Bannocks and all other early people were just following trails that had been formed by bison, elk, sheep and other animals for uncounted millennia. Wildlife utilize the easiest, most efficient ways to move between resting and feeding areas.

These five to six month
old calves were standing in
the sagebrush steppe typical
of the Hayden Valley.

The one on the left was probably born
a few weeks earlier than the other or is
perhaps a bull calf which is bigger than a
female calf. Born the previous April or
May these two five month old bison calves
have changed from their rusty brown
spring calf color to the dark brown-black
of adults. They will not be adults for
another four years or so. By then the
difference in size that a few weeks of age
makes will no longer exist.

Lush stands of grasses,
sedges, and rushes
grow and cover the
wet floor of the
Hayden Valley along
the Yellowstone River.

The valley was once flooded by an arm
of Yellowstone Lake and is covered by
fine grained clay and silt which makes
the soil nearly impervious to water.
Trees do not do well in this soil, but the
result is a rich source of forage for grazers
and browsers. Bison do very well in this
habitat in spite of the high cold environment. These bison are part of the largest
herd of bison in Yellowstone, the
Mary Mountain herd.

In this photograph a pronghorn antelope doe is standing beside her fawn of the year.

The fawn is four to five months old. The doe always gives birth to twins, and typically only one or neither of the twins will survive to even three months of age. The pattern of white bands on each pronghorn's neck is as unique as a finger print. Does have horns, but they usually are not very big. The fawn looks very healthy, and since it has survived until October, it has a very good chance of living through its first winter.

These two male fawns were sparring, although they were too young to know why yet.

They can be identified as males because they each have a black spot at the base of their jaws. Even though they are less than five months old, they already have horn buttons that are a couple of inches tall. As adults they will likely grow horns from a foot high up to twenty inches high. They tapped the tops of their heads together a few times and pushed back and forth briefly before going off to eat or amuse themselves in some other way.

The pronghorn antelope is the only animal with horns that are shed annually and that have two points each.

The prongs that are the extra points extend toward the front from the center of the main stem. The only land animal that can run faster than the pronghorn is the African cheetah. Pronghorn are wary animals and readily take flight on their delicate thin legs. Their eyesight is exceptional, and they can run for miles at speeds of up to fifty miles per hour. This small buck was carefully watching another buck off in the distance. Because he was smaller, he didn't seem to want to challenge the other buck and after a short time went back to grazing. In a couple of years he may be more aggressive and might try to maintain a breeding harem of does.

Pronghorns mate in September and October after bucks claim a small herd of does as their harem.

Mature bucks travel around trying to chase off the dominant bucks from their harems. Sometimes they succeed, sometimes they linger near the harem watching for a chance to sneak past the dominant buck and mate, and sometimes they move on looking for another herd. This large buck was nowhere near a harem, but he was in great condition, so I suspect he was traveling while on the lookout for a small herd of does.

To the west across Blacktail Deer Plateau, along the Gallatin Range, the warm light from the evening sun shines through the smoke from the 1988 fires.

The distant haze and orange color are normally rare in the clear, clean air of the Yellowstone Plateau.

Elk are gregarious animals.

The cows stay in small groups with calves and young bulls through most of the year, from late winter through the summer. In late August and early September the mature bulls, which have been in bachelor herds, scatter across the Park and start to claim the herds of cows for access to mating. This five month old calf had not seen much of these big bulls in her life, neither had she seen nor heard such outrageous noise, commotion, and fury from her fellow elk.

The mating season or rut of elk is a frantic, noisy affair.

One of the first things the bull elk needs to do is to look and smell right. Large antlers are apparently important. Big antlers can intimidate smaller or less aggressive bulls and help keep them away from the cows. Bulls will rake their antlers across mud and grass, often after first urinating on the spot. They seem to want to smear the musky mud all over themselves. The odor is strong because even though I have a poor nose, I can easily tell when I am near one of those muddy wallows or muddy elk. The little spot on his brow tine is a smelly muddy ornament, from his furious desire to be attractive to the soft eyed cows in the nearby meadow.

At five months of age, this bighorn lamb was no longer nursing but still stayed near its mother. The ewe was lying in the late autumn grass chewing her cud and nonchalantly tolerated the lamb's investigations. The lamb sniffed around the mother's head and horns and then scratched her nose on the tip of the ewe's right horn.

The Lower Falls of the Yellowstone River flows over dark brown rhyolite which is hard and very resistant to erosion. The lip of the falls is the point where the basement rock of rhyolite has not been chemically altered by geothermal activity. A waterfall of 309 feet stands in spectacular glory at the head of a multi-colored canyon that reaches a depth of nearly a thousand feet and extends for 18 miles. A surprising number of trees sprout and grow on unstable, dry, sliding, rocky and dusty canyon walls. Clinging to the dizzyingly steep eroded slopes, they endure. With no hospitable grassy rich soil to sustain them, they never get very large but demonstrate the tenacious force of life.

Looking north from the Artist Point Lookout, you can see a small section of the Yellowstone River below. The lodgepole pines that grow on the sides of the canyon all seem to have a difficult time surviving. The dead pine has stood for many years and twisted at least three complete spirals from its base to the top. The weathering and aging of the wood has created beautiful swirls of amber, charcoal, and gold.

The common raven has a rather misleading name, because its intelligence is uncommon.

Ravens are some of the smartest birds in the world; 37 different calls have been identified and it has been demonstrated that they can count. They have a significant capacity for play; in addition, they use objects as tools. They are extremely noisy and aggressive, and are a critical part of Yellowstone's ecology. The usual sound we associate with ravens is the "kronk" sound. They also have other calls ranging from tapping sounds, burbling sounds, clicks and pops, to high bell like notes. Some of the sounds carry great distances. The raven on page 31 is making a burbling sound and needs to raise his shoulders and thrust out his throat in order to do it. "If men had wings and black feathers, few would be clever enough to be ravens," said Henry Ward Beecher.

The Yellowstone River flows 400 feet below Artist Point between the steep walls of the Grand Canyon.

The surface of the river was reflecting the clear autumn sky, slightly backlighting the rippling cascades that stretched across the water. By exposing for the bright surface the film recorded this abstract detail but was blind to the much darker walls on either side.

Canada geese are distinctly beautiful, partly because of their black heads and crisp white cheeks.

A loop of white extends from behind their eyes completely under their chins. Autumn bird migrations are defined in North America by the movements of the high "V" shaped flocks of Canada geese moving south. Their normal flight speed is about forty-five miles per hour, although they have been observed flying at sixty miles per hour when chased. These speeds are particularly impressive considering their nine pound average weight.

Gold is the dominant color of Yellowstone's autumn vegetation.

These sedges in the wide marsh at the mouth of Pelican Creek grow lush and tall early in the summer. As creek and lake levels drop, the ground, which had been flooded and recharged with nutrients, dries and supports the dense stands of vegetation. Curing to the rich golds of autumn, these sedges become a dense reservoir of food for the winter bison herds that congregate here. Pelican Creek empties into the broad blue jewel of Yellowstone Lake, just a mile or so east of the lake's outlet at Fishing Bridge.

A herd of thirty cows and calves grazed up to the west bank of the Yellowstone River one morning in the Hayden Valley.

This bison cow thought they were ready to cross the river, so she waded in and swam most of the way across. When she reached the shallow opposite side of the river, she stopped and looked back wondering why the rest had not followed her. She stood alone in two feet of water. While she waited, four Canada geese became interested in her. They swam upstream to within six feet of her and hung in the current. The cow may have disturbed some vegetation on the river bottom that floated up in reach of the geese; they were picking at something on the river's surface. After about ten minutes, the cow swam and waded back to the west side of the river where the herd had decided to stay and spend the rest of the morning.

Just before sunset, the
widely diffused light filters
through the nearly cloudless
sky coloring the distant
ridges lavender.

Along Crystal Creek, this small
stand of aspens grows near a marshy
area and provides cover and food
for a wide variety of animals.

The Lamar River was
named after Lucius
Quinctius Cincinnatus
Lamar, the Secretary
of the Interior from
1885-1888, in honor
of his work to preserve
and maintain the Park
after the scandal of
Superintendent Robert
E. Carpenter's tenure.

The northeast corner of the Park is
drained by the Lamar River and
comprises some of the wildest and most
spectacular country in the ecosystem.

After the sun sets, for a quarter of an hour, the land sometimes becomes tinted a muted blue.

Distant ridges, close to the sky, hang on to the warm light from above, but the cooler blue builds and intensifies from the valleys, reaching up to color the hillsides. All other colors gradually disappear as the light dims until just the blue overpowers everything coloring this twilight time darker and darker until black arrives, the color of night.

Two bison bulls were walking across Swan Lake Flat in the dimming light, moving to a place where they would rest after grazing in the evening.

Just a few days before it would be full, the moon was above the eastern horizon and some thin cirrus clouds. The early evening light was dim enough so that the moon stood out from the darkening sky. It is easy to overlook the moon when it is in the sky during mid-day. Often in the evening we remark that the moon has just come out when it has been hanging above us for hours, outshone by the sun.

The sky was becoming the deep blue of twilight with the afterglow of a warm sunset still burning up from the western horizon.

The shadowed dim light at this time of day was not illuminating obvious things; instead it was suggesting what was there. The light faded in a retreat to the inky black above. Old Faithful was only a wisp contrasted against what was left of the day's light.

Traveling at a slow walking pace, this small herd of bison grazed and moved to the west end of the Lamar Valley.

The grass was cured to a rich, nutritious, and satisfying state. The weather was cool. The bugs were gone. Deep winter was still months away, and September felt as though it should go on forever.

(pages 42-43)

The sun had just come over the trees and was melting the frost on the light colored grass. This big, frost covered bison bull turned broadside to the sun to expose as much of himself as possible to its penetrating warmth. His dark brown hair absorbed most of the sun's heat, and as the frost and moisture evaporated, a wispy line of steam danced along the top of his back disappearing into the air above. His exhalations produced a puff of steam from each nostril out and down into the grass in front of him. Moisture in the air was visible here only while making the brief transition from a warm place to the cool enveloping morning.

Ultimately all fighting or sparring is a test of strength and will.

Even in play, there is an underlying element of competition. The bison rut or mating season is in late July and August. They still spar to maintain their order of dominance; most of these confrontations are settled without much effort but with a lot of dust. Once in a while with two evenly matched individuals the exchange might escalate into an aggressive fight. They rarely go so far as to draw blood, but this kind of serious pushing and shoving between 1500 pound bulls must cause a few bruises.

Mature bison bulls are obviously powerful creatures.

Their massive hump and shoulders make the animals appear to rest primarily on their front feet. Because their weight is concentrated toward the front, they are able to pivot and turn quickly. Autumn is the perfect season for them because they are able to graze peacefully during the cool days and build up extra fat for the harshest season soon to come.

At the top of the one
way road on the upper
terraces of Mammoth
Hot Springs is a traver-
tine formation called
Orange Spring Mound.

Active since at least the 1880s this spring
is growing up and to the west and at the
present rate will eventually bury the road.
Park geologists estimate that the Mammoth
Hot Springs complex produces about two
tons of rock per day so the shapes and
size of these features can change daily
and are one of the most dynamic rock
formations in the world.

Sinter is a hydrated form
of silica and is common in
the geyser basins.

The shapes of the small terraces and
scalloped ridges originate from the cooling
and evaporation of thermal water and the
escape of carbon dioxide gas. The sometimes brilliant colors in the thermal features
come from algae, bacteria and other rare
and little studied thermophiles. Minerals
such as iron oxide (red), iron sulfide
(gray and black), sulfur (yellow), and
arsenic compounds create multicolored
features. I think the most interesting life
form that lives here is a group of organisms
called *cyanobacteria*. They were one of the
first life forms to depend on the sun's
energy for life, and they produce free
oxygen as a byproduct. The success of
the prehistoric *cyanobacteria* is a major
reason we have an oxygenated atmosphere,
which now supports many other life forms
including humans.

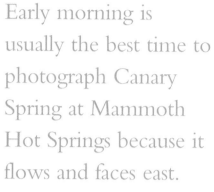

Early morning is usually the best time to photograph Canary Spring at Mammoth Hot Springs because it flows and faces east.

The old Jupiter Terrace, now dried up for nearly twenty years, still has the nice white and gray texture of travertine, and the rapidly building formation of Canary Spring is adding hundreds of tons of the same rock up against its south edge. This dynamic formation of hot spring deposits changes every day, so these landscapes are never repeated due to the infinite possibility of any unrestrained force.

The runoff channel from Doublet Pool is a copper green and rusty gold from the sinter under the diamond shapes of the tepid, thin glaze of moving water.

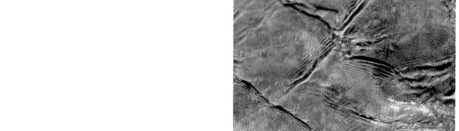

Electric Peak,
in the Gallatin
Range, dominates
the northwestern
corner of
Yellowstone.

It was thought to be the highest point
in the Park at 10,982 feet until someone
finally checked it out in the 1930s. The
highest peak is Eagle Peak at 11,358 feet
in the Absaroka Mountains southeast of
Yellowstone Lake. Looking northwest
from Swan Lake Flat early in the morning,
the luminous yellows and golds of the
tall marsh grasses and rushes contrast with
the blues of the sky and the distant peak.

Great blue heron and
Canada geese

During the last ten minutes of the sun's direct light on the land, shapes are often revealed that were entirely unnoticed before.

The simple line of the smooth edge of a gentle slope was highlighted in front of the deep shadow of a far mountain. Each grass stem stood briefly in a narrow radiant glowing curve of light.

These clumps of great basin wildrye were highlighted by the last low sweep of light before sundown.

The rabbit brush's fuzzy seed heads and dense cover create an interesting contrast to the tall thin reach of the three clumps of grass.

The grass family is called Gramineae.

These are plants that have narrow leaves with parallel veins and small inconspicuous flowers. The stems, usually round, are mainly hollow except where the leaf is attached. The many species of grasses mature all summer long. Some produce seeds and mature in June, while others do not mature until September. The growth succession of each grass follows a pattern of moisture and heat requirements. Each species prefers a specific soil, surface and subsurface moisture, and has certain shade tolerances. Each will also tolerate diverse levels of grazing impacts. This is a very adaptable group of plants that thrive in virtually all environments. Mature fall grasses in Yellowstone are predominately yellow and gold, but some have tints of

 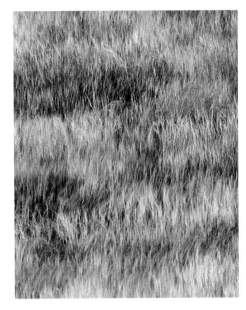 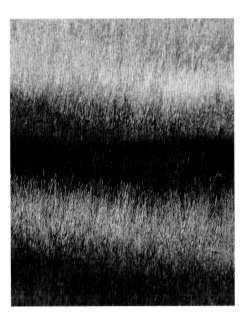

red, blue, green and orange. Sighing and softly hissing, grasses bend and flutter in wavelike shapes as fall winds push through them, picking up seeds, broken stems, dust and the warm smells of September. When the chlorophyll in plants is no longer needed at the end of the growing season, the underlying colors of the grasses that appear are usually yellow and gold. The colors scattered across the hillsides become a mosaic of shapes determined by species variation, soil and moisture differences, orientation of the stems from wind and other disturbances, and the angle and quality of the light striking them. I find that the communities of montaine grasses under the infinite variety of light and shadow become a constant source of beauty.

Walking and hunting across the dry, brittle grasses during a cool autumn morning, this coyote was aware of all the other sounds around him in addition to the rustlings of potential mouse prey.

A raven set up a racket off in the distance behind him, and he briefly stopped, turned to look, and swiveled his ears to catch the sound better.

Walking across the Hayden Valley, this coyote was hunting for rodents, mainly mice and voles.

The lush growth of vegetation from the previous good spring and summer seasons had created a thick cover for these rodents, making it harder for the coyote to catch them. Most of the time he came up with just a mouthful of grass, or he had the rodent with some salad attached.

Amethyst Creek is a small perennial stream flowing off the north slope of Specimen Ridge into the Lamar River.

It originates in a cool, damp, and densely forested bowl. One main source of the moisture for the creek is the huge snowdrifts which accumulate over the winter on the leeward side of the top of Specimen Ridge. The drifts will sometimes survive until late July with their moisture trickling down into the creek or soaking into the aquifer that supports the numerous springs below. Part of this seldom visited oasis is highlighted here by a late afternoon beam of light scrimmed by dark promising rain clouds.

The vocalizations of coyotes vary from barks to howls, to squealing yips, to yowls.

If a coyote wants to produce a full complement of sounds, he needs to throw his nose up high into the air and open his mouth wide. This posture must create the best shape in his throat to make sounds that will carry for miles in the right conditions. For such a little dog, he can make a lot of racket.

The sinter cones or tubes of
Monument Geyser Basin stand in
a very unlikely spot.

Formed under water, they are near the
top of a steep ridge over 600 feet above
the Gibbon River. Similar spires recently
found under Yellowstone Lake were
formed around hot water vents. The
theory for the existence of Monument's
features is that the hot water vents were
once under water backed up behind a
glacial dam during part of the Pinedale
glacial event which occured between
seventy and thirteen thousand years ago.

Castle Geyser has two phases during a major eruption.

The first is the water phase, lasting about fifteen minutes, followed by the steam phase, which lasts for another twenty minutes or so. During the water phase, bursts of hot water are thrown up to eighty feet in the air in a steaming fountain above a massive cone of rock. The water rises into the air, slowing to the instant of weightlessness. Round drops sparkle and spin just before they collapse back into the steam and pulse of the succeeding burst.

A vertically building cumulus cloud like this one,

especially with the classic anvil shape, means that precipitation is likely. Discerning observations of clouds and wind are a very good way to predict weather. I am primarily captivated by their shapes, however. These huge masses of moisture somehow create a feeling of sturdiness with a velvet surface. I used to imagine as a kid that I could climb to the top of these clouds and jump and bounce down their billowy soft terraces.

Unless they build
vertically, cumulus
clouds, are an indication
of fair weather.

These clouds plus the gentle breeze and
warm temperature meant the rest of the day
would be pleasant and invited me to rest
under the juniper tree on the ridge top.

The ridge on the east side of Gardners Hole has some small stands of aspen trees.

The afternoon light made the yellow leaves glow and illuminated the texture on the southern slopes of Electric Peak. A polarizing filter saturated the color in the vegetation by removing the shine on each individual leaf and darkening the blue sky, making the clouds and the peak stand out in greater contrast.

There had been a light snow the night before, nearly covering the ground with a haze of white in the grass.

Looking over the tops of some yellow aspens, I watched four bison bulls walking along the old road to what was once Yancey's hotel site. He operated a rustic hotel here near the old road from Mammoth to Cooke City from 1884 to 1903. During the summer the present concessionaire carries people on horseback and in horse drawn wagons to an evening steak cookout and cowboy singalong around a fire. By October the picnic crowd had left for the year so the bison were no longer bothered by people looking for an outdoor experience.

The snowshoe hare received their name because of their large hind feet.

These feet enable them to more easily run across the surface of snow giving them an advantage over their predators. They live in the high or northern forests where snow is on the ground more than half the year. They are hares, not rabbits, which means they give birth to young that can open their eyes right away, are covered with hair, and are up and running about in a few hours. Snowshoes also change color twice a year. They are white in the winter and brown with white feet and legs from early spring to late autumn. Snowshoe hares are one of the creatures that have cells with pigment in the cytoplasm called chromatophores which can be dispersed or concentrated thus changing the color of the animal.

Hidden under the bark of the lodgepole pine, insects may be burrowing in the living layer of wood.

Pine bark beetles lay eggs under the bark, and when the eggs hatch, the larvae live and grow by eating the nutritious sap filled cadmium layer. This tree had died several years earlier, and the bark had dried up and fallen off, exposing the abandoned trails of the hungry, growing larvae. Here we can see how one grew as it fed from its appearance in the lower left to the upper right. If you listen carefully on quiet warm days, you might hear the faint nipping sounds of these pale ivory white insects munching along under the bark. These sounds are often what woodpeckers use to locate their own lunch.

Aspen is naturally a forest forming tree which usually creates dense practically pure stands with many trees coming from one common root system.

The bark is smooth, grayish white or pale green, and commonly covered with a white powder. The black round and diamond shapes scattered up the trucks are scars from old small branches. Browsing animals or claw marks from bears climbing in the trees will leave distinctive black scars, too.

Cirrus clouds like these are ice clouds and usually indicate good weather.

It was a warm autumn afternoon and the brightly colored aspen trees standing under this indicator of more good weather made the day even nicer.

The queen of the white faced hornet starts building a symmetrical round nest in the spring and rears the first workers who continue these tasks so the queen can just lay eggs.

The nests are elaborate overlaying shells of paper made by the hornets chewing wood into pulp and spitting it into thin layers. Hornets feed on other insects and nectar. The nests can get over a foot in diameter and contain over 10,000 insects. This colony was living in a dense thicket of wild rose bushes. The nest was surprisingly difficult to see even though it was ten inches in diameter. In the winter it will disintegrate. In the spring the new queen will start another nest nearby.

The North Fork fire of 1988 had completely burned this stand of Douglas fir near Tower Junction.

Lush tall stands of grasses and annual vegetation appeared the first few years after the fire. The most conspicuous post-fire vegetation was a biannual aptly named fireweed. It appears in wild profusion the first few years after a fire when it occupies the bare open soil, now free of competition from the trees, brush and grass. It is called a pioneer species because it is one of the first plants to appear after a fire or other disturbance. The plant produces cotton-like seeds the second year, and the leaves turn a bright red in the fall adding vibrant color and texture to a solemn landscape of towering dead trees.

Eating rose hips and other
vegetation, this male cinnamon
black bear was busy
clambering over the fallen
timber along Elk Creek.

Rose hips grow on thorny stems, so he
had to be careful stripping the mealy
apple-flavored fruit from the thin bushes.
Rose hips are mainly seeds, so there
might not have been a lot of nutritional
gain. Volume was the key to gaining
weight in his hyperphasia stage before
he went into hibernation.

A mule deer fawn could die
from many things in November.

There was no sign of a struggle, so the
fawn probably died from some disease,
parasite, or starvation. The coyote found
this fawn and now had a terrific source of
food for days. He fed on the nourishing
protein for twenty minutes or so, rubbed
his face in the grass nearby to clean off the
blood and left. I waited for a few minutes
until he returned with another slightly
smaller coyote which must have been
his mate.

Gardners Hole is in the
upper stretch of the Gardner
River drainage just south
of Electric Peak.

The Gallatin Mountains border the west
side of this valley or "hole," named after
an early fur trapper named Johnson
Gardner. Gardner is the second oldest
place name still in existence in the Park,
the name Yellowstone is the oldest of all.

The steely piercing whistles of bull elk carry across the park from early September until mid October.

The grunts and other sounds of elk are beautiful too, but these sounds don't carry as far. The poised intensity of the individual elk during his whistle or "bugle" is illustrated here in these two images. Capturing this classic stance is the main reason many photographers come to Yellowstone every autumn.

The cretaceous shales on the north end of Mount Everts are highly eroded and have little vegetation, because of the low rainfall in the Gardiner area. These features illustrate the processes that tear down mountains. The four nearly parallel draws which carry water down off the steep slope are cut into a "V" shape by the rapid tumbling of runoff from rainfall and snow melt. The afternoon light brushes sideways across the normally nondescript, nearly monochromatic landscape, and illustrates the complex textures of the hillside.

(pages 74-75)

Standing near the northwest corner of Yellowstone, Electric Peak is just under 11,000 feet tall. Gardners Hole and Swan Lake Flat both lead up to its southern slopes. Here, one September evening, a small herd of mature bull bison quietly walked through the lush golden grasses looking for a place to rest for the evening.

These bighorn rams were each at least six years old and are referred to as "full curl" rams. This means that their horns spiral up, back, and around forward, completing at least a full circle or curl. The tips of their horns are often broken off, broomed, or rubbed off. Sometimes the horns grow into their line of vision, and the rams rub off the tips so that they can see more clearly.

A full curl ram, like this one, is usually at least six or seven years old.

During the mating season in November, when they run full tilt into each other, occasionally they hit one another with the tip of their horn instead of the base, shattering the tip into broken fibers. This is called a broomed horn, like the bristles on a broom.

Deep, impassable ridges cascade down to the Yellowstone River in the canyon below Inspiration Point.

During the Absaroka volcanics fifty million years ago, there were extensive lava flows near the East Entrance.

The plastic hot rock must have flowed and surged in small lumps up to an edge and cooled like blobs of mud stacked on top of each other. This basalt would have been heated to thousands of degrees to become soft, but we can still imagine the lumpy fire-hot stuff slowly oozing and climbing over the previous lumps and perhaps plopping down over the edge like handfuls of wet mortar.

Pikas are a member of the lagomorph order that includes rabbits and hares.

In autumn, pika are very busy collecting vegetation. They store it in piles in their homes in the matrix of talus slopes and rock piles. They do not hibernate. Since pika live in the higher elevations with heavy snow cover, they need a handy large food supply to carry them through the winter.

Forms and shapes found in nature are infinitely variable
yet we want to classify each into broad categories.

This travertine rock might be called lacy
especially with the algae and bacteria growing brown and black in the water flowing
across it. The formations at Mammoth Hot
Springs grow quickly. In the most active
parts they visibly change from day to day.
These delicate swirls and fingers of rock
invite close inspection, and the sounds of
the moving water add an extra incentive
to stay and watch.

Spiders have been making tools
for much longer than we have.
Their efficient, adaptive webs are common
across Yellowstone during the three milder
seasons. We usually don't see them, which
is why they work so well; they are made to
be nearly invisible. We usually notice them
only when we brush into them, which is
the same accident a small insect makes,
and it is usually its last mistake. In the cool
early morning, when the dew and light
frost is still on the vegetation, the webs are
also covered with the same light moisture.
A normal stand of grass and brush reveals

hundreds or even thousands of unique little
traps or nets that run across the infinitely
variable twigs and blades of vegetation.
Each impossibly thin web strand is coated
with frost crystals or minute globes of water,
as if someone had hung out her finest jew-
elry for all the neighbors to admire. This
twinkling, glowing treasure makes the webs
sag from the impossible weight of such
unbelievable riches. The spiders who made
these displays remain patiently invisible
waiting until the jewels silently evaporate,
then they repair their webs, and they
become tools for making a living again.

Angel Terrace near the top of the formation at Mammoth
Hot Springs has become very active in the past ten years.

Hot water in this spring, laden with calcium carbonate, is flowing off the upper east-facing slope of the Mammoth Terraces flooding out into stands of fir and pine. This tree was first killed by the heat of the water and was being slowly buried by the embrace of flowing rock. Minute particles of dissolved limestone were gently but firmly building a solid tomb, perfectly fitted to the curves of the trunk and each branch.

Hanging under a light twig and attached to the trunk of a pine tree, this large classically shaped spider web had captured some of the faint cool moisture drifting down the Hayden Valley during the night.

The accumulation of this moisture left hundreds of rows of drops on a single web suspended ten feet off the ground. The water remained there until the sunlight finally burned through the fog. After shining directly on the web for just a few minutes, the web was dry and nearly invisible again and still intact.

Yellowstone is the southernmost point in the Rocky Mountains where great gray owls live.

They are North America's largest owl and are most common in the northern boreal forests, living in the woods next to open meadows. They roost and nest in heavy timber and hunt in the grassy areas nearby. Like all owls, they fly silently, but what is amazing to me is how easily they fly through heavy timber with a wing span of up to 52 inches. I have never seen them even break a small twig as they swoop through the trees. They hunt primarily by sound. This great gray had caught a pocket gopher in the grass, flown about 300 yards into an area recently burned by the fires of 1988, and landed with her meal on the end of a large charred fallen tree. I set up my tripod and long lens beyond the other end of the tree. During the ten minutes I photographed her, she stood with the dead gopher clutched in her feet. She looked up in the sky at a raven, tipped her head down slightly and closed her eyes for a half minute as if she were sleepy, and quietly looked off in different directions. Something made a sharp sound behind me; she thought it was me making a move to steal her gopher. She bent down towards me, flared out her feathers and seemed to say "Don't touch my gopher." She then picked it up and flew silently away.

Tilting its head to help pinpoint the sounds of a small rodent busy in the grass, this owl waited intently on a low perch until it was sure of its prey.

It flew out above it, stalled, tipped forward, and fell into the grass with its feet smashing into the deep grass in order to squeeze the life out of the startled, unfortunate mouse. When the disheveled, crashed owl felt that the mouse was dead, it wiggled its head down into the grass and plucked the dead mouse out head first. After looking around for a quick check to see if anything nearby might steal it, the owl made a couple of jerks of its head to arrange the mouse and drop off stray grass stems. It flipped its head up and swallowed the mouse head first in four gulps.

They will sit for hours watching and listening over a meadow, waiting for a rodent to accidentally reveal itself. The owl is primarily listening for the rustling sounds of its prey which is trying to make its own living by feeding on seeds and other vegetation. With supersensitive ears the owl must have a phenomenal amount of auditory information coming in. Its job is to sort out all this racket and only commit its efforts to a decent meal. Bugs, wind noise, and who knows what all must be filtered out. Tipping its head once in a while, the owl must decide if a noise is the right frequency and intensity and hope that it comes from little furry feet or a fuzzy face.

Coyotes travel around opportunistically watching for a chance to catch or scavenge something.

In autumn there are a lot of chances to catch mice and voles in the thick grass. To catch rodents a coyote walks carefully and attentively, listening and watching for his prey. He usually locates it by sound. The rodent rustles the grass when moving, crunches seeds and vegetation in its teeth, or makes sounds moving dirt. When a coyote hears one of these sounds, he will stop walking and listen to see if it continues. If the rodent continues to move about unaware of him, the coyote will try to get as close as he can without alerting it. Often the coyote will look at the ground immediately in front of him to see where to place his feet so he doesn't crunch any grass or twigs and scare the rodent. While easing his way forward the coyote listens intently, tipping his head back and forth to pinpoint the spot where the rodent is working. When the coyote gets close enough, he usually tenses his body and gathers his feet under him before pouncing. He will often leap up into the air and come crashing down into the grass, trying to pin the rodent down with his front feet. He immediately bites into the grass to grab the creature so it won't wiggle away. If he catches a small rodent in his mouth, usually he bites down hard, picks it up, crushes it in about three chewing gulps, and swallows it whole. If he misses, he sometimes gets a mouthful of grass or dirt. Then he might stand watching to see if the rodent makes a dash away from his feet, so he can make a second quick jump at it. If he realizes it has escaped, he gets moving after another one.

Wildlife browse the leaves of the aspen and if the winter is severe will sometimes eat the woody stems and the white bark.

The subsequent scarring from the ungulates' feeding is a rough black bark up to two inches thick. Here the original white bark is surrounded by scars.

Badgers are the most beautiful member of a whole family of strikingly beautiful creatures called mustelids.

Mustelids are all aggressive predators that have each evolved to fill a diverse array of niches. They range from river otters which catch fish in fresh water, to pine martins which catch squirrels and chipmunks in heavy timber, to skunks which catch mice and insects in grasslands, to a creature that can dig like a backhoe after ground squirrels and rabbits—badger.

I came upon this badger one pleasant, quiet day in October while hiking near Gardners Hole. Usually a badger runs away from people surprisingly fast on short little four inch legs. This individual and I studied each other for a couple of minutes. Then he settled back into the grass where I had first seen him. I watched him for at least 45 minutes while he slept. If people had wondered what I was doing, I could have told them I was working, learning a lot about badgers. It was easy for me to be patient because the day was perfect. I had not had a chance to watch a badger since I was a kid on our cattle ranch.

After a while, he moved around and dug briefly in some loose dirt and disappeared down a nearby hole for a minute or so. When he emerged, he sniffed the breeze coming from the west. Before he took off in the tall grass, he sat down and gave himself a good bath. He cleaned the insides of his hind legs, scratched under his front legs and chin, cleaned his belly and yawned and shook himself thoroughly. He had cleaned, combed, and wiped most of his spectacular black and white striped face and his beige and rust colored belly looked fluffy, soft and fresh. Even his long curved claws were clean and ready to move some dirt.

This trumpeter swan stood on its right leg on a sub-merged rock and delicately dipped its beak into the water without taking a drink, creating tiny ripples on the glassy surface.

Maybe it was just moistening its tongue. While I watched, it stood and created a clear reflection on the mirror surface of this small kettle lake in the Lamar Valley.

The Latin name for trumpeter swan is *Cygnus buccinator.*

A closely related bird, the tundra swan, is also native to North America, and looks nearly identical but usually has a yellow spot in front of each eye at the base of its black beak. Positive identification is done by examining the shape of the windpipe within the breast bone. The trumpeter has a pronounced extra half circle loop that the tundra swan does not. This trumpeter swan was resting on a rock that was barely exposed above the surface of the pond. For the first year of their lives trumpeters are light gray. During their first molt, in their second summer they produce white feathers and their beaks are black. This individual's legs and feet were still a fleshy pink color so it was probably just one and a half years old.

Diagonal lines of tree tops, mountain ridges, and the sagebrush and grass covered slopes in the Hayden Valley were delineated by the humid haze lying over the Yellowstone River Valley.

The subtle colors here inspire a sense of calm which was the mood during that quiet morning.

Because this trumpeter swan stood on its right leg for over half an hour, I had to remind myself that it did have another one.

The toes of its left foot are visible behind its tail in the second photograph. The steady grace of its actions and calm watchfulness made me think that no human ballet dancer would be able to maintain this kind of posture for that long. The swan nestled its head along its back and closed its eyes.

After resting about fifteen minutes, it raised its head and preened. I moved around in front of the bird to photograph the graceful arc of its right leg, supporting and balancing the heavy roundness of its body. It tipped its head to the right, a left leg appeared, and it scratched its head.

I thought it would then stand on both legs, but instead it tucked its left leg back up into its feathers. Twisting its head sideways it watched a raven sail across the sky and disappear over the ridge beyond. Then the swan delicately stretched out its left wing until it nearly touched the

surface of the water. The smooth, gentle strength of this motion was combined with its counterbalancing neck and body above the one thin supporting leg. When I left, the swan was still standing on its right leg calmly observing the surrounding pond and grassland.

101

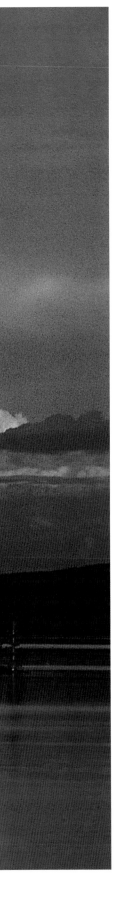

Evening thunderheads were building up above the Absaroka Mountains along the east side of Yellowstone Lake.

The magnificent clouds climbed thousands of feet up into the cooling air and hinted that we might have a noisy night of thunder and lightning with wind blown rain flung across the lake's surface and into the creaking, moving forest.

Rapidly changing shapes in this cumulus cloud illustrated the power of the high altitude winds moving these tons of moisture.

Just as interesting and beautiful as a mountain or prairie landscape this cloud formation changed radically in just a few minutes. The nice light appeared and vanished during that few minutes, too.

A clump of ticklegrass was lit by the last warm glow of the evening sun. It was bent by the prevailing west winds of summer to tip toward the calm surface of Trout Creek.

Most of the seeds had fallen out of the heads, but the thin tall stems still showed the strength of the slender, waving grass.

The gold light at sunrise was diffused by a light fog above the Yellowstone River.

The tall grass stems are simple, sharp structures extending up, over the graduated soft textures of fog and water surface.

Sunsets are hard to predict.

Dramatic light seems to occur only when a number of things come together at the time the sun is at or near the horizon. To make an interesting sunset photograph there almost always has to be a dramatically lit cloudscape. Light bouncing off objects on the land and/or water can make the composition even more beautiful. The gold light beam reaching toward me on the surface of Yellowstone Lake creates a strong sense of depth and space. The dark cloud above the sun creates a ceiling which helps push the gold sun back to the distant western shore of the lake.

To see the most dramatic light it is best to be out just before sunrise.

The sun may light up the clouds above the horizon just before it appears, and this light will illuminate the landscape in its own broad, varied and diffused color. Here, along the north shore of West Thumb, the colors of the predawn clouds reflected on the still surface of the lake, but the gravel bar and trees remained black silhouettes.

Sometimes the brief light of a gold sunset appears to infuse everything with a liquid intensity.

The seed heads of bluejoint reedgrass seem to be part of the source of the light, not reflectors. The light burns in a warm glow that invites a soft caressing touch and contact. We might expect the gold edges to brush off like magic dust on our hands and make them glow, too.

Warm light during a brilliantly lit sunset seems to attract our admiration and awe the same way a campfire stimulates our meditative dreams.

The movement of drifting clouds and orange, red, and yellow changing light causes many of us to stop in our busy lives and look and hold our breath in contented amazement.

Yellow-bellied marmot

Bison cow

Dark-eyed junco

There are at least a couple of theories about why birds and mammals yawn.

One is that they are tired. An involuntary yawn seems to increase blood circulation, to stretch some muscles, and to increase the volume of inhaled air and exhaled carbon dioxide. A yawn sometimes seems to be a form of stress relief. It can be a signal to others nearby that this creature intends no harm, or it can be a submissive gesture. I have observed many individual animals

(pages 108-109)

Lying in the cool shade of a large Douglas fir this bull was relaxing in a perfect bug free afternoon. He stuck his tongue out and twisted his ears during the abandonment of a large, intense yawn.

Pika

Great gray owl

California gull

yawning and when it accompanies stretching and settling behavior, I think it must be some sort of muscle release for relaxation.

The eyes are usually closed in a relaxation yawn, whereas they are open in a stress relief yawn. The relaxation yawn seems to occur only when the animal feels safe, and it puts the individual at a brief, temporary point of vulnerability.

Tree swallow

Coyote

Elk cow

Trumpeter swan

Badger

Cottontail rabbit

Minerva Terrace faces
east and this backlit
image was made in the
first two minutes after
the sun rose over
Mount Everts.

Cool autumn air makes the steam from
the hot water lift in delicate waving
forms that climb up out of the pools of
water and move like dancers on the
travertine formations.

This image was made when
the moon was full, so the sky
appears black.

The moon is so bright that film cannot
see texture on the moon at the same
time it records the last dark blue of the
disappearing day. Smoke and dust in
the air make the moon orange. Usually
Yellowstone's air is so clean the moon
appears white.

Under high clouds and flat
light I waited for sunrise in
the Hayden Valley at the
mouth of Alum Creek.

It looked as though the sunrise was
going to be dull. I had had good luck
in this spot before, so I waited. When
the sun came over the ridge I had about
two minutes of beautiful warm light.

During those two minutes I raced back
and forth, shooting with several lenses,
putting the sun behind clusters of different
trees and using different reflections in the
foreground. It was over so quickly, that I
began to wonder if it had ever happened.

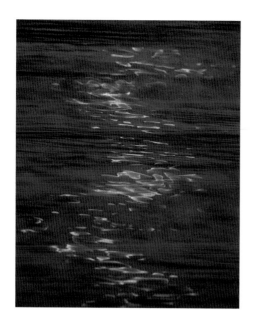

Rising in its usual powerful and commanding way, the moon appeared above the crest of the Absaroka Mountains on the east side of Yellowstone Park.

From the west shore of the lake, a reflected moonbeam shimmered across the undulating and shivering surface of the water. It appeared to me as a living silvery darning thread connecting me to the perfect globe of our moon.

Walking through the sagebrush and grasses of the Hayden Valley before sunrise, this bison bull appeared for about thirty seconds.

He came out of the dim blue haze and walked past me without stopping to consider why I might be there. He walked on into the haze which silently closed around him. While he was briefly in my sight, I could see the high thin plume of steam from Sulfur Mountain rising up into the delicate light of sunrise.

Hunting along the west side of the Yellowstone River,
this coyote was having pretty good luck in the early morning.

He walked briskly along, stopped abruptly, made a sneaking move up to a promising sound and leaped into the air to pounce on a small rodent. In the four jumps I saw the coyote make in twelve minutes or so, he caught three mice or voles. This was his third leap when he was silhouetted against the steamy smooth river surface. A successful wildlife photograph freezes a creature in a continuing story. While this photograph represents only a small fraction of a second in this coyote's day, the instant this photograph was made should illustrate the story for this coyote and for other hunting coyotes, too.

When the Yellowstone River falls off the edge of the hard outcrop of rhyolite at the top of the Lower Falls, the mass of green water starts to come apart. The surface breaks up, and the wind pulls more and more white spray off as the column of water drops faster and faster. The column is bent and stretched as it falls, becoming more white than green. Where the mass of water crashes onto the rock 309 feet below, it hits with tremendous force and ricochets out in all directions at a cold hurricane storm speed. The fractured spray is pushed up and out drifting downstream for hundreds of yards as a ragged cloud of rain, creating a small microclimate of nearly constant heavy moisture.

All animals have to sleep and dream.

Bull elk

Bighorn sheep

When they are comfortable and feel safe, mammals may rest and sleep. They become totally relaxed and sometimes even make snoring, snuffling sounds. They usually open their eyes about every ten minutes, and without moving immediately close them and return to sleep. They seem to be aware of sounds and smells and will react to them. If there is no threat they will fall back to sleep quickly.

Trumpeter swan

As the rain drifted slowly
below the sunlit edge of
a small thunder shower,
a faint rainbow lingered
for a minute or less.
When the shower evaporated, the
clouds closed over the sun, and the
sky started to close up for the night.

The most successful wildlife
photographs illustrate what
an animal's life is like.
Animals are very mobile. In still photographs this motion is usually difficult to
convey. When this elk calf walked down
a steep slope, I made the exposure at
about 1/8th of a second and "panned"
or followed her movement in a diagonal
track. The slow shutter created a fluid
sense of motion and hurry in this image.

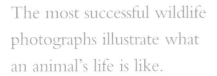

The early morning sun was
sweeping across the gold, frost
covered grasses and forbs in this
small riparian area in the sagebrush
steppe of the Hayden Valley.
Patches of light were manipulated and
shaped by the low bands of fog rising from
the nearby Yellowstone River. Mists rose
from the dark bare ground as the heat
from the low sun melted the frost and
carried the moisture up to join the gently
drifting fog. All this movement, the fog
and mists, and the light play made the
quiet morning even more magical because
movement usually generates sounds. Yet
all was still this late autumn morning.

Fog is common around Norris
Geyser Basin in the autumn.
So are elk. Several small herds live in the
grassy parks from Twin Lakes to Gibbon
Meadows. This bull was traveling along
the edges of the meadows, in and out of
the trees, looking for cows that were not
attended by other bulls larger than himself.

Above 6500 feet this
rain storm had been a
wet sticky snowstorm,
coating the trees and
grassy ridges above the
floor of the Lamar
Valley with much
needed moisture.
The warm ground at the lower elevations
pushed the moisture into the air where it
formed low clouds which drifted slowly
down through the draws and canyons.

One of the things that is so fascinating about the travertine terraces at Mammoth is the way their scale can be so confusing.

Without an explanation, this photograph could easily be confused with an aerial shot from thousands of feet in the air of a landscape of sedimentary rock formations with plateaus and cliffs hundreds of feet high. Instead the cliffs are two to twelve inches high, and the green is from microorganisms not forests of juniper.

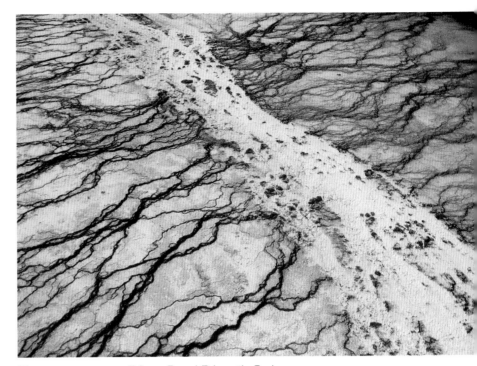

Sinter terraces, runoff from Grand Prismatic Spring

Pool and travertine lip,
Mammoth Hot Springs

Downstream, about 1/4 mile below Sheepeater Cliffs the Gardner River runs over a hard ridge of basalt.

During autumn the rough broken river bed creates a wild array of white water. Before the U.S. Fish Commission stocked this part of the Gardner River in the late 1890s there were no fish above Osprey Falls which is about two miles below this rapids.

Crystal Falls was named by the Langford–Washburn party in 1870.

P.W. Norris, the second superintendent of Yellowstone, gave special attention to this falls in 1878, building a viewing platform and a bridge across Cascade Creek above the falls. Visitors now might notice it when looking at the Upper Falls from the viewing point near Uncle Tom's Trail.

The Lower Falls, like all other significant features of Yellowstone, exhibits a wide array of moods, shapes, and forms depending on the season, light, weather, and other natural forces.

I like this image of the Lower Falls because it shows the shape and character of the rock at the lip of the falls due to low water during an exceptionally dry year. This photograph was made in October of 1988. Just a small fraction of the normal volume of water is flowing over the falls, and the deep notch on the east side is obvious while the west side is nearly dry.

During one cool morning, a layer of fog lay in the Yellowstone Valley from the lake to the base of Mount Washburn.

While the light was soft and flat in the fog, the sharp ridges of the canyon below the Lower Falls appeared and disappeared as the fog moved downstream.

Near the head of Obsidian Creek there are numerous small thermal springs and fumeroles.

The creek is warm its entire length and in some places too hot to put in your hand. Grasses and rushes stay green year round in the warmest sections along the banks and in the water.

All ungulates, and some other mammals such as horses and donkeys, exhibit a behavior called flehmen or lip curl.

Without a sound, they open their mouths and pull their upper lips back after smelling the urine of another individual. Males are testing whether the urine is from a female in heat. Only during the initial period of the estrus cycle, when the female is ovulating, will most mammals, including elk, mate. Just before sunrise this large bull was walking behind a group of cows and tested the urine of one of the cows. He held his nose high, for about five seconds and made no sound. Bugling is an entirely different posture. When a bull bugles, his mouth is rounded and the upper lip is not pulled back. The little clump on his left brow tine is dirt and grass which remained after he scraped his antlers across the grass.

Obsidian Creek gently flows through a boggy area near the Grizzly Lake Trailhead.

There are many standing dead and fallen trees where the creek had flooded and killed them due to its heat. This small pool was formed from water backing up behind a fallen submerged log. Early morning light illuminated the clump of ticklegrass and highlighted standing tree trunks across the stream, causing their reflection to mimic the color of the grass.

These grasses and rushes are in a scattered stand of dead lodgepole pine that had been killed by floods of hot water from Obsidian Creek.

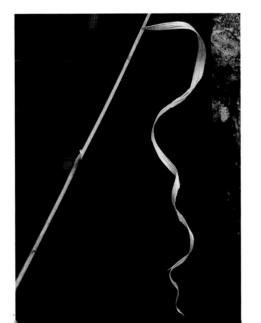

A single stalk of basin wild rye leaned to the right in front of a granite boulder.

As this leaf dried, it curled and twisted like an inverted wisp of smoke.

From the top of Lake Butte high above Yellowstone Lake, the Teton Range is visible to the southwest.

Here Mount Moran rises on the other side of the ridge line that is the Continental Divide. Frank Island, the largest of the seven islands in Yellowstone Lake, is seen in cool shadow below the soft light of sunset.

Grasses and rushes thrive in marshy spots near thermal features.

The damp, moist and warm ground is ideal for their growth.

Willow Park, in the northwest quadrant of Yellowstone, is great autumn habitat for moose.

Dense stands of willow extend for three miles along Obsidian Creek. Moose browse these willows by putting their mouth around a small bundle of branches, pulling on them, and letting the branches slip through their mouths, stripping the leaves off just like stripping grapes from a bunch. This cow had spent the spring and summer here mostly by herself. During the rut the big bull appeared and stayed until the cow came into estrus. While he waited, he stayed close to her, often moaning and calling in the strange sounds familiar to moose.

In Norris Meadow,
every autumn a small
resident herd of elk
cows and calves takes
up residence.

The grass is thick and nutritious, so they
stay until the heavy snows of winter drive
them away. The elk are attracted to some
of the forbs in the meadow too, such as
this Canada thistle that the calf had bitten
off. Trying to avoid the stickers and break
it into smaller pieces, she twisted her head
around and up and down hanging onto the
thick end with her lips and teeth. Unable
to break it apart, she spit it out and moved
on to find something more palatable.

TOM MURPHY

Tom Murphy's photographic passion and specialty is Yellowstone Park. Since 1975 he has traveled extensively within its 3400 square miles, hiking thousands of miles and skiing on dozens of extended overnight trips in the backcountry. He has skied across the park twice, once on a 14-day solo trip. Two things motivate him to travel carrying a heavy backpack: a desire to see Yellowstone's wilderness backcountry and to photograph the behaviors of free-roaming wildlife and the colors, shapes, and textures of the land.

His photographs have been used, both editorially and commercially, in numerous regional, national, and international publications. Clients include: *Life, Architectural Digest, National Geographic, Audubon* and *Time. Newsweek, The New York Times Magazine, National Geographic Adventure, Esquire,* and others have sent him on assignments.

His first book, *Silence and Solitude, Yellowstone's Winter Wilderness,* won a 2002 Montana Book Award. The video, *Silence and Solitude,* produced by Montana Public Television, earned an Emmy nomination for Tom's photography. *The Light of Spring,* the first book of a four-volume set entitled *The Seasons of Yellowstone,* was printed in 2004.

He donates the use of his photographs to environmental groups, supporting their efforts to preserve wildlife and wild land. In 1984 he graduated with honors from Montana State University with a Bachelor of Science in Anthropology. He lends his backcountry skills to the Park County Search and Rescue team, which he helped to organize in 1982. He was the first person licensed to lead photography tours in Yellowstone Park and operates, with his wife Bonnie, Wilderness Photography Expeditions. He also teaches workshops and special seminars for camera clubs, nature centers, and institutions such as the Yellowstone Association and Montana State University.

WILDLIFE PHOTOGRAPHY ETHICS

Good wildlife photography ethics assume that all creatures have a right to go about their lives without interference from us. The best wildlife photographs illustrate what an animal's life is like. How does it make its living? How does it interact with its environment? How does it respond to others of its own species and to different species? How does it play? What are its feeding, traveling, resting, and other behaviors like? If a photographer disrupts an animal's actions, not only is he distracting and modifying the animal's life and potentially causing it harm, he is not going to photograph natural behavior. I am not interested in photographing an animal's response to me. I want to show the beauty and uniqueness of a creature's daily life.

To avoid disturbing an animal's daily routine, it is best to use long telephoto lenses. An automobile is one of the best blinds from which to photograph in national parks. You must observe and understand wildlife's behaviors. Learn to read their body language and if your presence is disturbing them, even 300 yards away, leave at once. I think of myself as a visitor in their living room and try to be a humble and considerate guest.

ACKNOWLEDGEMENTS

A sincere thank you is always necessary for any successful project.

Thank you to Bonnie for her continued support, help, and encouragement in my photography and for many hours carefully rereading and correcting my writing.

To Edie Linneweber for help proofreading.

To Adrienne Pollard for her wonderful work assembling and presenting 25 years of my autumn images in this book.

To the wild lands of Yellowstone and to the innocent beauty of all the creatures who live there.